917.29

Books are to be returned on or before
the last date below

THE CARIBBEAN

Cas Walker

Evans Brothers Limited

Published by Evans Brothers Limited
2A Portman Mansions
Chiltern Street
London W1M 1LE

First published in Great Britain in 1988 by
Hamish Hamilton Children's Books

Maps by Janos Marffy

The illustration of Mary Seacole on page 30 is by Michael Simpson. It was
reproduced bycourtesy of the City of Birmingham Education Department.
© City of Birmingham Education Department.

New edition published 1992
Reprinted 1997

Typeset by Cylinder Typesetting Ltd., London
Printed in Spain by GRAFO, S.A. - Bilbao

ISBN 0 237 60189 3

Acknowledgements

The author and publishers would like to thank the following for permission to
reproduce the photographs: Stephen Benson Slide Bureau contents page, 14
(right), 23; Anne Bolt 12 (left), 20 (left); Bruce Coleman Limited 11 (right), 21,
29 (left) Sullivan & Rogers; Compix title page, 18, 20, 23 (right), 24 (right)
Collin Hanno, 25, 26, Dave Saunders, 27 (right), 29 (bottom right), 31 (bottom)
Dave Saunders; Robert Harding Picture Library cover, 8, 12 (right), 14 (left), 15,
16, 17, 19, 20; The Hutchison Library 9 (left), 10 John Wright, 11 (left) Philip
Wolmuth, 19 (right); B. Régent 22 (left) Philip Wolmuth, (right) John Wright,
27 (left) John Wright, 28, 29 (top right) Prue Rankin Smith, 30 (right) Philip
Wolmuth; Jamaica Tourist Board 17 (left); Mansell Collection 7 (top); Mary
Evans Picture Library 7 (bottom); Panos Pictures 13 Marc French, 24 (left);
Popperfoto 31 (top); Rex Features 9 (top right) Jose Alfonso; Ronald Sheridan 6

Cover A beautiful beach near Speightstown, Barbados.
Barbados is a beautiful island with white sandy beaches
and rolling countryside. It has a hot, breezy climate and
attracts a lot of visitors.

Title page Carnival time in Trinidad. The costumes are
always spectacular and some people spend the whole year
designing and sewing their outfits! Carnival costumes
usually follow a theme or depict fantastic creations.

Opposite Fishermen bringing in their catch on the island
of Martinique. The Caribbean Sea is full of many varieties
of fish.

Contents

Introducing the Caribbean

The Caribbean islands are spread over many hundreds of kilometres in the Caribbean Sea. Some of these islands are large masses of land while others are little more than small peaks of rock. The Caribbean covers an area of about 230,000 square kilometres, between Cuba in the west and Barbados in the east. The islands are known throughout the world for their beautiful scenery and sunny climate. Over 30 million people live in the area. The size of the population on each island varies. Some tiny islands are uninhabited or have a very small population for example Dominica, Antigua and Grenada. Other larger islands like Cuba, Jamaica and Puerto Rico are densely populated.

Mainland connections

The Caribbean region has historical and political connections with parts of Central and South America as well as the UK and France. The countries of Guyana, Guyane and Surinam on the South American continent are part of the Caribbean region. Surinam is part of the Kingdom of the Netherlands while Guyana and Guyane are independent countries. Belize in Central America is also part of the Caribbean territory.

The people

The islands were originally populated by Arawak and Carib Indians but the majority of the Caribbean people today are the descendants of people from Africa, Europe and Asia. Most people are descended from Africans who were taken to the islands over 350 years ago. Other islanders are descended from Chinese, Indians, Syrians and Lebanese. Many Jews migrated to the islands from the 17th century and European settlers arrived in the 16th, 17th and 18th centuries. The Caribbean today is truly a mixture of many peoples.

Transport

Cars, trucks, and vans are plentiful in most of the large towns and cities. Many people use bicycles and motor scooters and travel by public transport or on foot. In really rural areas donkeys or mules are used for transport or to carry heavy loads.

A rail service is possible only on the larger islands. Cuba was the first country in Latin America to have a railway system, and it now has the largest network in the Caribbean.

Many of the world's airlines fly to the Caribbean and because some of the islands are far apart, local air services are also needed. The distance between Barbados and Jamaica is over 1800 kilometres. There are several Caribbean airlines, including Air Jamaica, Cayman Airways, BWIA (British West Indian Airways) and Cubana. The air service carries mail and freight as well as passengers.

Sea transport is used mainly to carry cargo between the islands. Large ocean liners and yachts cruise the islands carrying tourists and pleasure seekers.

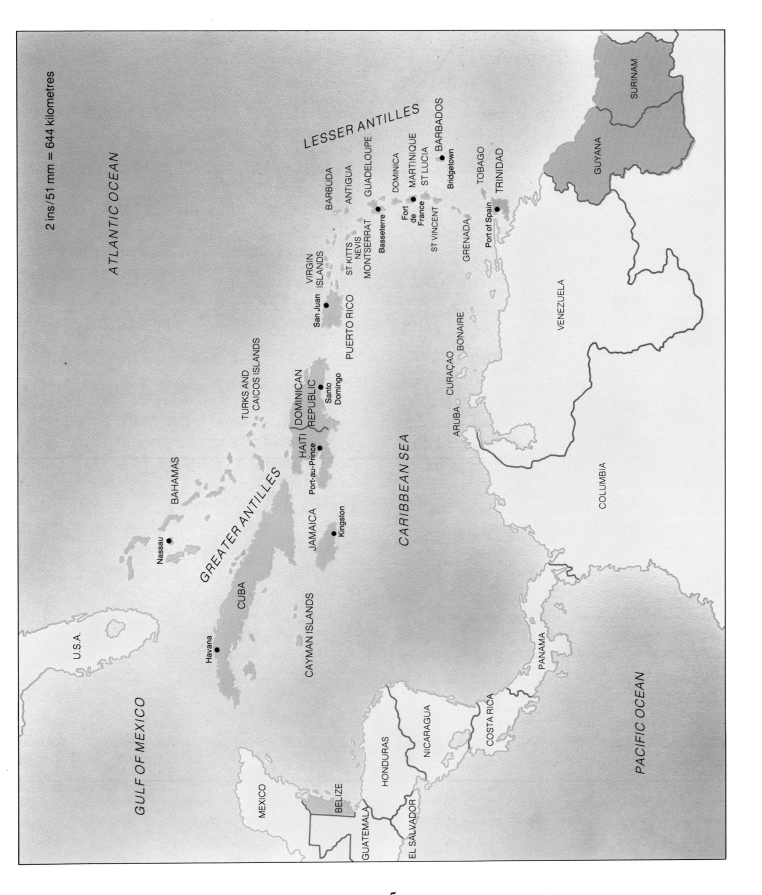

2 ins/51 mm = 644 kilometres

ATLANTIC OCEAN

LESSER ANTILLES

BARBUDA

ANTIGUA

GUADELOUPE

DOMINICA

MARTINIQUE

Fort
de
France

ST LUCIA

BARBADOS

Bridgetown

TOBAGO

TRINIDAD

Port of Spain

ST KITTS

NEVIS

Basseterre

MONTSERRAT

ST VINCENT

GRENADA

VIRGIN
ISLANDS

San Juan

PUERTO RICO

SURINAM

GUYANA

VENEZUELA

CURAÇAO

BONAIRE

ARUBA

COLUMBIA

TURKS AND
CAICOS ISLANDS

DOMINICAN
REPUBLIC

Santo
Domingo

HAITI

Port-au-Prince

CARIBBEAN SEA

BAHAMAS

Nassau

GREATER ANTILLES

JAMAICA

Kingston

CUBA

CAYMAN ISLANDS

Havana

U.S.A.

GULF OF MEXICO

MEXICO

BELIZE

GUATEMALA

HONDURAS

EL SALVADOR

NICARAGUA

COSTA RICA

PANAMA

PACIFIC OCEAN

Exploring the past

Nobody knows exactly when the first people came to live in the Caribbean islands. Archaeologists have found ancient remains which suggest that there were settlers there 7000 years ago.

Early inhabitants

The earliest known settlers were the Siboney. They came from the South American mainland. They hunted and fished for food, but very little is known about them. About two thousand years ago a group called the Arawaks became the main settlers. They made their homes in villages on the larger islands. They grew yams, cassava, potatoes, maize, tobacco and pineapples – some of these are Arawak words.

Later the Carib people began to occupy the region. They developed a successful trade in fish between the islands. The Caribbean is named after these settlers. Descendants of the Caribs still live on the islands such as Dominica. We know that the Arawaks and Caribs made pottery and dug out cotton trees to make canoes. They also liked dancing and made musical instruments from gourds and pebbles. We can see evidence of their everyday life from the drawings they made on rocks and in caves.

New arrivals

When the Spanish explorer Christopher Columbus arrived in the Caribbean in 1492, he was met by Caribs and Arawaks. Columbus describes in his journal how these people taught him and his crew to survive on the islands. Columbus thought he had reached eastern India and he called the area the Indies. Other Spanish explorers followed Columbus to the islands thinking they would find gold. Europeans from other countries came soon after. Battles for control of the islands were fought by European kingdoms. Some islands changed ownership many times between Spain, France and Britain. The variety of languages spoken in the islands is part of this history.

An Amerindian carving, made over 400 years ago.

Slaves being punished in a treadmill.

Slavery and rebellion

The European settlers did not find much gold. But they soon discovered that they could get rich by growing crops. They were cruel to the Arawaks and Caribs and forced them to work as slaves in the fields. The Europeans became wealthy because they paid their slaves nothing at all. Arawaks and Caribs resisted slavery and many died as a result. Others died because they caught European diseases. The population became so low that the Spanish went to Africa to capture new slaves. During the 17th and 18th centuries millions of Africans were forced to leave their homes to work as slaves on plantations in the Caribbean.

The lives of these African slaves were so terrible that many ran away or even killed themselves. The slaves tried to rebel against their masters. One great rebellion took place in 1804 in St Domingue, a French colony. Over a million slaves joined together to set up the Free Republic of Haiti. After this other people began to realise how evil slavery was and gradually it was abolished.

New governments

When slavery ended the wealthy European landowners could not make as much money as before and many left the Caribbean. The islands became colonies ruled mainly by Britain and France. Some influential Caribbean people began to think that they should be independent. In the 1930s trade unions began to develop, political parties started to grow and many people in different islands were given the right to vote. In 1944 Jamaica was granted internal self-government. In 1945 the same happened in British Guiana and British Honduras. By the early 1950s the movement for independence had grown, with some islands in favour of joining together and forming a federation of islands. But in the end each island wanted their own government and by the early 1960s some finally gained independence for example, Jamaica in 1962.

An old painting, showing European ships arriving in the Caribbean. They used to explore the islands in search of treasure.

Cuba

Cuba is the largest Caribbean island. It is situated about 56 kilometres south of the Florida coast and covers an area of 110,900 square kilometres. Nearly all the other Caribbean islands can be fitted into Cuba, and because the island is long and narrow, no one lives very far from the coast. Over ten million people live in Cuba and nearly two thirds of the population live in small towns. The people speak Spanish with Creole, the local language made up from African and European languages. Cuba produces petroleum products and sugar and tobacco for export. Cuban cigars are famous throughout the world.

Havana
Havana is the capital city of Cuba with a population of over two million people. It is the chief manufacturing city and has an international airport and a sea port. The port at Havana harbour handles about three quarters of the island's imports.

History
Arawak people had already settled in Cuba when Columbus and his crew arrived there in 1492. The Spanish took over the island and made it an important base for exploring and capturing other islands. The fine harbours provided a good shelter for pirate and treasure ships and the Spanish found gold there. But by the 17th and 18th centuries it was sugar that was making the settlers rich. By the 19th century Cuba was the world's largest producer of sugar. Another crop which helped to make the Spanish rich was tobacco. These crops needed a lot of labour and the

Havana, the capital of Cuba, showing the central and old parts of the city. It has many modern shops, hotels and housing estates.

8

Spanish used African slaves because they did not have to pay them. Slavery was abolished in Cuba in 1886.

The Spanish ruled Cuba until 1898. It became an independent republic in 1902 after a war between Spain and the United States. The island became a centre for pleasure seekers and gambling. Many people from the USA moved to Cuba. In 1959 a revolution took place led by a lawyer called Fidel Castro. He and his supporters introduced a new style of Communist government. They wanted a fairer system where wealth was more equally shared amongst the people. They felt it was wrong that a few Cubans were very rich while so many were very poor.

President Fidel Castro the Communist leader of Cuba.

Developing country

Cuba, like many Caribbean islands, is a developing country. The government under Castro has set up many programmes to help young people. In sport Cubans have achieved world success in athletics and gymnastics. Education and training is very important. The government has built many new schools and hospitals and provides a welfare service to help people get cheap medical treatment. Some young Cuban volunteers offer their services and skills to other Caribbean islands. Doctors and construction workers have also been sent to African countries. Before the 1959 revolution unemployment was high. This has improved, but Cuba is still poor and the political changes in Russia have meant that Cuba can no longer rely on financial support from the former USSR.

The library building of Havana University. The tank on the right of the picture is part of a monument.

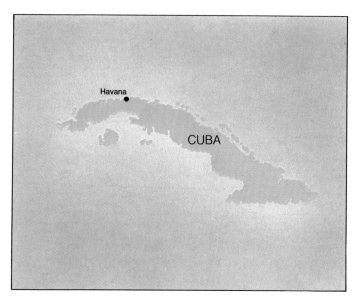

Haiti and the Dominican Republic

The second largest island in the Caribbean is the only one that is divided into two separate countries. It covers 76,400 square kilometres and is the most mountainous island in the Caribbean. Pico Duarte in the Dominican Republic is the highest peak in the Caribbean at 3175 metres.

Two countries

The two countries are Haiti, in the west, and the Dominican Republic in the east, which is twice as big as Haiti. When the Spanish came to the island in the 16th century they called it Hispaniola. Later the French took over the western part of the island which is now Haiti. The name Haiti comes from the Arawak word 'Hayti' which means 'the country of many mountains'. Port-au-Prince is the capital city.

Haiti was ruled by France until 1804 when black slaves, led by Toussant L'Ouverture revolted and began to rule themselves. It was not until 1821 that the Dominican Republic was established. The capital city is Santo Domingo.

A varied countryside

Although they are on the same island, the two countries are very different. Few people live in the Dominican Republic, while Haiti is densely populated. The Dominican Republic is full of beautiful scenery. It has high waterfalls, winding rivers and colourful fishing villages. Inland there are lots of

A busy market in Port-au-Prince the capital city of Haiti.

mountain areas to explore. There are natural forests of hardwood such as mahogany and rosewood and there are also large pine forests. But exports of timber are now restricted and the government has also set up national parks to protect the environment. Agriculture is carried out on a large scale with sugar-cane and bananas grown on plantations. Industries include gold mining, iron ore and amber mining.

Haiti is a country damaged by many internal wars. Political unrest has made life hard for the Haitian people. They live in small scattered settlements on hillsides throughout the island. Farming is on a small scale, with crops grown mainly for local use. Very little food is exported.

French and Spanish influence

The Spanish became very rich from trade in the Dominican Republic and some of their wealth can be seen in the monuments and buildings. There are many cathedrals, such as the Cathedral of Santa Maria de Menor where the bones of Columbus are said to be buried. The cathedrals also contain Spanish paintings and other treasures. The people speak Spanish and Spanish Creoles. Santo Domingo has a Spanish style with wide avenues and grand buildings.

Haiti is still influenced by France and some Haitians speak French as well as French Creole. Following the slave revolution of 1804, the French ordered the islanders to pay compensation and in return granted them independence.

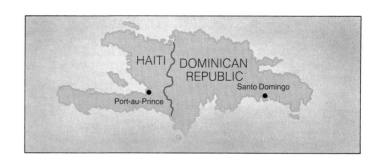

Santo Domingo Cathedral with a statue of the Spanish explorer Christopher Columbus. The Dominican Republic was said to be the island that Columbus loved best.

Toussaint L'Ouverture

Toussaint was a famous black hero who helped his people to win their freedom from slavery. Toussaint was born a slave in 1743 on the French part of the island, St Domingue (Haiti). Although he was a slave, his master was not too harsh and allowed him to learn to read. Toussaint learnt about France and Africa, and soon realised how unjust slavery was. He and other friends decided to fight against the slave owners. Toussaint helped to organise a slave army. They planned the best ways to defeat their masters. Toussaint was a brave and clever soldier and eventually he was able to lead his country to victory over the British and French armies. Haiti became the first black republic in 1804. Toussaint was eventually tricked by the politicians and arrested. He died in a French prison.

Toussaint L'Ouverture

Jamaica

This island is famous throughout the world. It lies 56 kilometres south of Cuba and 62 kilometres west of Haiti, covering an area of 10,991 square kilometres. Today, there are about 2.4 million people living in Jamaica. The Arawak name for the island was 'Xaymaca', meaning 'land of wood and water'. Jamaica is made up of three main regions: the mountain ranges, the coastal plains and the limestone plateau. The Blue Mountains is the highest range. The Spanish were the first Europeans to capture the island in 1655.

Living in Town

Kingston is the capital of the island and is situated on the southern coast. It has a fine harbour and an airport just outside the city. Many people move into the area looking for work while others migrate to Canada and the USA. The main streets are busy lively places with offices, shops and banks. There are also parks, libraries, cinemas and theatres. Other places of interest include the Royal Botanical Gardens, the museums and art galleries. Visitors can explore the old Spanish town and Port Royal, a famous old harbour and port.

Some people live in big houses in the hills outside the city, others live in smaller town apartments. Kingston is a growing city with a growing population and some people find it difficult to find a suitable home. Some areas of the island are very crowded with poor quality dwellings.

The Blue Mountains is the highest mountain range in Jamaica with a high point of 2256 metres. Some of the world's finest coffee is grown in this region.

A shanty town outside Kingston. About a quarter of Jamaica's population live in the capital.

Fishermen pulling in their nets on Jamaica's south coast.

Rural Jamaica

Life in the countryside is very different from life in the city. Many country people have a smallholding, a little land where they can grow food and keep animals. There are few industries or factories to provide work. Many local people are employed in the tourist industry. Tourists from North America and Europe visit the northern coastal areas and the famous beauty resorts. Places to see include bathing spas, old plantation houses and inland towns like Mandeville. These towns are cool because they are high up in the mountains. People in the country areas usually make their own entertainment and the pace of life is slower than in Kingston.

Language and heritage

The languages of the Caribbean developed from contact between Europeans and Africans. The African people brought their own languages such as Ga, Twi and Fanti. Europeans brought Spanish, English and French. Chinese and Hindu are also spoken. The language which developed in Jamaica is usually called Creole, but it is also known as Patois or Dialect. Many Jamaicans understand Creole. Children are taught English at school. Creole has been mainly a spoken language but now there are books where Creole is used. Louise Bennet is a famous Jamaican poet who writes in Creole. Other writers such as Linton Kwesi Johnson, in England, became popular using Creole for poetry and songs. Bob Marley is world famous for reggae music and his songs which tell about political subjects like slavery or racial discrimination. He was awarded the Order of Merit by the Jamaican government shortly before he died in 1981.

Many different peoples have made their homes in Jamaica. They have brought with them a different cultural background and heritage. This may explain why the Jamaican motto is 'Out of Many, One People'.

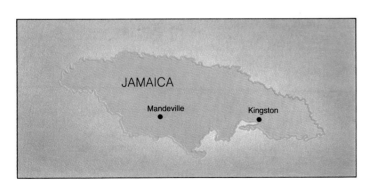

Jamaican language – 'Patois/Creole'

Creole	English	Creole	English
patu	owl	cotta	head cushion
nyam	eat	bulla	small cake
juk	poke	duppy	ghost
bwoy	boy	oono	you
facety	cheeky, bold	macca	thorn, prickle
bankra	covered basket	pone	cake, pudding

Puerto Rico

Puerto Rico, which means 'rich port' in Spanish, is situated 105 kilometres east of the Dominican Republic. It is the most easterly of the large islands and is 63 kilometres long and 64 kilometres wide. The population is about 3½ million. The island is a dependency of the USA. Puerto Rico was once covered with tropical forests but most of these have been cleared for farming. There are three small islands which depend on Puerto Rico – Vieques, Culebra and Mona.

San Juan
San Juan is the capital of the island. It was founded and developed by the Spanish. The old part of the city is built in a Spanish style with large white buildings and gardens. This part of the city is full of history with narrow, winding streets. A famous historical landmark in San Juan is Castillo de San Felipe de Morro. The new part of San Juan has many offices and factories and the island's most modern port. There is also an international airport and many luxury hotels for visitors.

San Juan the capital city showing some of the large luxury hotels.

The Castillo de San Felipe de Morro in San Juan. This is one of the many forts built by the Spanish to keep out other European adventurers.

San Juan is full of history, and many of its streets are narrow and winding.

Luquillo beach, Puerto Rico. Many tourists visit the island and cruise ships from Europe and America stop regularly.

History and development

The Caribs had already settled in Puerto Rico when the Spanish arrived in 1493. They fought fiercely to defend their island from the Spanish invasion. But they could not fight against guns, so they were defeated. Other European countries tried to take over the island, but the Spanish held on to it until 1897. The United States went to war with Spain in 1898 and eventually took over the island which then became a colony of the USA.

Puerto Rico remained mainly rural until the 1940s when industrial development began. A governor of the island decided to create more jobs for the people by bringing factories and tourists to the island. This project was called 'Operation Bootstrap'. Puerto Rico now has many industries and factories which produce a variety of products such as clothes and medicines.

Places of interest

There are a great many things to see on this island. It has beautiful beaches and many forests with wild flowers and ferns. There is a beautiful National Forest and Nature Reserve in the Luquillo Mountains, where there are many tropical trees. Along the South Coast is a famous beach called La Parquera. The phosphorescence makes the water here glow brightly at night and it is called 'The Bay of the Living Light'.

Puerto Rico still has many old Spanish buildings, including cathedrals, churches and monasteries. There are also modern buildings such as the University of Puerto Rico at Rio Piedras and the government buildings. Just outside San Juan is an American basketball stadium and a pleasure park next to the sea. There is also a horse-race track called Hipodromo de El Comandante. These places are very popular with local people as well as tourists.

Trinidad and Tobago

These two islands are the most southerly of the Caribbean islands and together cover an area of 5128 square kilometres. They are only a few kilometres off Venezuela on the South American continent. The two islands are quite different. Trinidad is a busy, modern, industrialised island while Tobago is quieter, more rural and very much smaller than Trinidad. The population of both islands totals about 1.2 million. Some people still call Trinidad by its old Caribbean name 'Iere' which means 'the land of the humming bird'. Tobago is sometimes called the 'Crusoe' island because it is so beautiful. Flowering shrubs, brightly-coloured birds, fruit trees and a sea rich with fish make it a tropical paradise. The island is particularly noted for its beautiful beaches, the best known is Pigeon Point.

The beach at Pigeon Point, Tobago. Across from this beach is Bucco Reef, one of the most beautiful in the Caribbean.

Multicultural society

Trinidad and Tobago are the islands which best show the great mixture of races in the Caribbean. Africans were taken to the islands followed by people from India and China who were brought as plantation labourers. Over a third of the population are of Indian descent. English, Hindi, Urdu, Chinese, Arabic, French Patois, English Creole and Yoruba are spoken in both Trinidad and Tobago. There are also people of different religions, including Christians, Moslems and Hindus.

Carnival

People from all over the world go to see the Trinidad Carnival which takes place each Spring. The costumes are spectacular (see title page) and music is a very important part of the carnival especially the competition between steel bands. The Trinidad Philharmonic Steel Orchestra tours and plays all over the world. Many young people in England and other countries learn to play the 'pans'. The calypso has also become world famous. This is a funny song which tells about local people or politicians.

Steel bands developed from the musical skills of African slaves. The instruments are made from old oil drums. They are cut, beaten into a special shape and marked to make musical notes.

Port of Spain and Scarborough

The capital of Trinidad is Port of Spain which has a population of about 59,200. This is a fascinating city to explore. The old town still exists, but most of Port of Spain is modern with a large manufacturing industry. It is also the island's chief cargo and passenger port. Many hotels, shops and banks serve the tourist trade.

The capital of Tobago is Scarborough. The city is small compared to Port of Spain because Tobago itself is only about 32 kilometres long. There is only one main street which runs through the centre of the city.

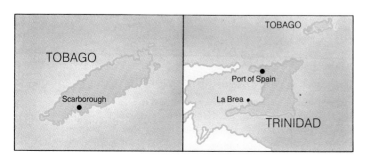

The Pitch Lake

In the South of Trinidad, at la Brea, there is a lake, not of water but of pitch. Pitch is a black, sticky tar used for surfacing roads. The lake is over 30 hectares in area and 60 metres deep. The Carib people have a legend about the Pitch Lake. They say there was a boy who used to hunt humming birds. This made God angry. He did not like to see his beautiful creatures killed. But the men in the village wanted the beautiful feathers of the birds to make headdresses. The boy and other young men carried on hunting. God got very angry and made the village and everyone in it sink into a black hole in the earth. This became the Pitch Lake.

Industries and manufacture

Trinidad is one of the most industrialised islands in the Caribbean. Oil refining is the most important industry and employs many people. Other Trinidadians work in factories producing clothes, chemicals, plastics and rum. A famous and unusual product is 'Angostura Bitters'. This is the extract from the bark of a tree used in medicines and to flavour cocktails. Important agricultural produce includes sugar, cocoa, coconuts, citrus fruits and coffee, very little is exported. In contrast, Tobago is mainly concerned with the tourist industry and with fishing.

Other islands

Barbados

Barbados is a beautiful coral island with a hot but breezy climate. It has white sandy beaches, rolling hills and great natural beauty. The population is about 254,000 about half of whom live in Bridgetown, the capital. The island attracts many visitors because of its beautiful scenery.

Barbadians, sometimes known as 'Bajans', are proud of the famous people who were born on the island: world class cricketers like Sir Garfield Sobers and Sir Frank Worrell whose picture can be seen on the Barbados $5 note, and writers like Edward K. Braithwaite.

The original inhabitants of the island were Amerindians. Spanish and Portuguese sailors visited the island but only the English began to settle in 1627. They cultivated the land, and cotton, sugar-cane and maize were the main crops. The landowners grew rich using poor labourers from England and later African slaves to work on the plantations. Visitors to the island can still see large plantation houses, windmills, forts and old churches. Barbados remained under British control until its independence in 1966.

Bahamas

These are a group of some 700 islands, 2300 cays (small islands, pronounced 'keys') and uninhabited rocks. They spread over about 11,400 square kilometres in the Atlantic Ocean. The capital is Nassau on New Providence Island. The population is about 245,000 and most people live in Nassau.

Every year thousands of tourists visit the Bahamas for sun, fishing and entertainment. The tourist industry is very important for the island's economy and provides work for many local people. Nobody pays income tax in the Bahamas so many wealthy people from the USA and Europe go to live there.

One of the most exciting events on the island is a festival held just after Christmas called 'Junkanoo'. People dress up in colourful costumes and parade around the streets.

A mineral called argonite has been found in the Bahamas. This is used to help in the production of steel and glass.

Part of a 'Junkanoo' costume. This festival has links with the African slaves who were brought to the Bahamas in the 18th century.

The Pitons, twin volcanic peaks on St Lucia. Volcanic activity on the island has produced many hot mineral springs and health spas.

The French influence on the island of Martinique is very strong with street cafés, French cars and French money.

St Lucia

This island belongs to the Windward group along with Grenada, Dominica and St Vincent. St Lucia covers an area of 603 square kilometres and has a population of about 145,000. The capital city is Castries. The English and French fought over the island for many years and the island still has a French atmosphere. Most of the people who live there today have African ancestors. St Lucia is a volcanic island, two of the highest peaks are Grand Piton and Petit Piton, both rising to over 610 metres. The two main industries are tourism and banana production. The island has many excellent beaches, good harbours and bays. Yachting and underwater sports are very popular.

Martinique

The beautiful island of Martinique is part of the French Caribbean. These islands are still under French control and the people are French citizens. Martinique covers 1100 square kilometres and has a population of about 360,000. French is spoken, as well as French Creole or Patois. The island is French in style with street cafés, French cars and French money, even the police are called 'gendarmes'.

Martinique is a rugged, volcanic island. In 1902 Mount Pelée erupted, killing about 30,000 people in the town of St Pierre. Martinique is also famous for its flowers and forest blooms. The Carib name for the island was 'Madinina' meaning 'Island of Flowers'.

The natural world

The Caribbean climate is almost an ideal one. Temperatures remain constant throughout the year between 25°C and 28°C. Most islands are warm and sunny, with a gentle cooling sea breeze. Rain falls throughout the year, most heavily on the mountainous islands in the east. Yet the Caribbean climate is not perfect; from July to October hurricanes can occur.

Hurricanes

Hurricanes are powerful storms which often cause devastation to many islands each year. Winds and torrential rain develop with such force that they damage buildings and crops and can last for several days. These tropical storms are given names such as 'Gilbert' (1988) and 'Hugo' (1989). Antigua suffered major damage and loss of life in 1995.

Earthquakes and volcanoes

The region has also been devastated by earthquakes. In 1692 an earthquake at Port Royal, Jamaica, killed over 2000 people. Most of the town was lost in the sea.

There are several active volcanoes in the Caribbean. Mount Soufrière, on St Vincent, often pours ash and lava out on to the hillside. At the Valley of Desolation, in the south of Dominica, boiling water gushes up into the air and steam rises from cracks in the earth.

(left) The Pouri tree – it grows very tall and produces yellow and pink flowers twice a year. (top) The hibiscus flower blooms almost throughout the year. (bottom) The fruit of the ackee tree contains a yellow pod that is a popular food in some islands.

Trees and flowers

The trees and flowers of the Caribbean make it very colourful. There are many beautiful flowering trees, like the blue jacaranda, the poinsettia and the poinciana. Some trees, like the frangipani and the hibiscus, are famous for their fragrance. Other trees provide food, for example, the breadfruit tree produces a vegetable about the size of a football. The soursop is another favourite Caribbean fruit.

(left) Trinidad is famous for a beautiful bird, the scarlet ibis. (top) This fruit bat is eating raw pawpaw. There are 25 varieties of bat in Jamaica and lizards are very common. (bottom) This is a Cuban ground iguana, the largest grows up to two metres long! (right) The streamer-tail humming bird, or 'doctor bird', is only found in the Caribbean.

Animals and birds

The wildlife on all the islands is quite spectacular. Trinidad has alligators, snakes, armadillo, ocelots (mountain cats), and an unusual rodent called the agouti. Most islands have large frogs, wild pigs and some small deer. Brightly coloured birds are everywhere, parrots, finches, toucans, flamingoes and many different kinds of humming bird. Tobago has a special nature reserve for the greater bird-of-paradise.

Conservation

The latest conservation development in the Caribbean is called 'Eco-tourism'. This policy encourages tourists to enjoy the beauty of the woods and forests and not just the beaches and coastal areas. Nature reserves have been set up in Trinidad and Tobago, Jamaica and Barbados. Many island governments are concerned about protecting their wildlife. They realise the importance of looking after their birds and animals. Some species are now officially protected, such as the Jaco parrot in Dominica. Some Caribbean countries attended a conference in Belize in 1991 to discuss ecology issues and tourism. Governments were asked to consider how the natural beauty of the islands can be protected for the future.

Industry

Agriculture is no longer the most important industry in the Caribbean. Crops such as sugar-cane and bananas are becoming less economic to produce. Exports of agricultural products now only account for a small part of the region's wealth. Other industries such as oil, bauxite and engineering are important and are still being developed. Tourism accounts for about 30 per cent of the region's annual income.

Oil

Trinidad is an island with many industries. It is also one of the oldest oil-producing countries in the world. Together with Tobago there has been quite a degree of wealth for the people because of the oil and petrochemical

A bauxite mine in Jamaica.

industries. The ABC islands of Aruba, Bonaire and Curacao have also developed an oil industry, although they do not process crude oil. They refine oil brought from Venezuela.

Bauxite

Bauxite mining is a very important industry in Jamaica, Guyana, the Dominican Republic and Haiti. Bauxite is a red soil that is mined and processed to produce aluminium, a strong, light metal that resists rust. Alluminium is used to make many metal goods, from kitchenware to aircraft. Most of Jamaica's bauxite is exported to the USA and Canada. It would be better for the island if there was a large aluminium manufacturing industry, but Jamaica does not have enough cheap electricity to do this yet.

An Amoco oil platform off the coast of Trinidad.

Fishermen weighing and selling their catch on a beach in Martinique.

Fishing

Fishing for food in the Caribbean goes back to the Caribs and Arawaks. Many fish have local names like goat fish, snapper, sea bream, jack fish, shad and parrot fish. Fishermen go out to sea in their boats at night or early in the morning. On many islands barbecued fish is sold on the beach. Barbados flying fish are a speciality and there is a special fleet to catch them. Cuba has developed a deep-sea fishing fleet with factory facilities on board for fish processing.

Turtles inhabit the Caribbean Sea and they are now protected. The Cayman Islands has a special turtle farm set up to breed turtles and return them to the sea.

Forestry

Most mountainous parts of the islands are covered with tropical forests. Finewoods like fiddlewood, mahogany and cedar are used locally for furniture making. Although many forests were cleared by early settlers there are still areas which support an industry.

Dominica and Trinidad have hardwood plantations of teak and Caribbean pine as well as mahogany.

On the mainland, Belize has a large timber industry. British settlers in the 18th century cut logwood for export to Europe. The logs were floated down river to the port at Belize City. Later a railway was built but now roads and large logging trucks are used. There are also forests in Guyana but only a few species are cut for export. There is now a growing awareness of the need to conserve the forests.

Other industries

Trinidad and Tobago the second largest producers of ammonia in the world. Most of the production takes place at Point Lisa Estate on the West Coast. Many islands have deposits of iron ore and there is some iron and steel production. Jamaica produces gypsum (a mineral) which is exported. There is also a small garment industry using locally made cloth. Light engineering and an electronic products industry exist on a small scale.

A timber mill in Belize.

Farming and food

The Caribbean islands are mainly agricultural countries. Most people work on the land, growing food for their own use or for export. In rural areas all the family – men, women and children – may help to cultivate crops. Most preparation and harvesting is done by hand using small tools. Some foods like yam, cassava, sweet potatoes and cocoa have been cultivated since the time of the Caribs and Arawaks. Many rural people have small plots of land near their home. They grow food crops and vegetables as well as citrus fruits and tropical fruits like paw-paw.

Caribbean farmers are usually small. Farmers might keep a few hens, goats and pigs and perhaps a cow for milk. Some might also grow green vegetables. Chicken meat is always in

Cattle being fed on a farm in Jamaica. On some islands such as Barbados and Antigua large-scale cattle farming is developing.

demand because it is a useful source of protein and poultry farming has developed on islands such as Jamaica.

Food for export

The islands grow foodstuffs which are exported around the world. The Dominican Republic grows many thousands of hectares of sugar-cane. On large plantations machinery is used for harvesting. Grenada, sometimes called the 'Spice Island', produces nutmegs and mace. Jamaica exports all-spice and ginger. Citrus fruits are also grown on some islands. Dominica grows limes which are exported for the manufacture of cordial. Many islands grow oranges, grapefruit and pineapples. Other special exports are

A small-scale banana plantation in St Lucia where half the island is given over to bananas for export to Europe.

coconuts, tamarinds (a fruit used for sauces) and many varieties of pepper.

Coffee and cocoa are two important exports. Jamaica's Blue Mountain coffee is often considered the best in the world. Other locally grown foods, such as ackees, soursop, breadfruit, mangoes, callaloo and pigeon peas, are tinned for export. These are bought mainly by Caribbean people living overseas.

Markets

Most Caribbean towns have a special market where fruit, poultry, meat, fish and sometimes cakes and bread are sold. In the country, markets may be set up along the roadside. Many islands have a straw market where hats, baskets and mats are sold.

Caribbean cooking

Caribbean cooking is drawn from a variety of cultures and each island has its own favourite

Caribbean markets are colourful, lively places. This is St George's Market in Grenada. How many different products can you see?

dish. Jamaica's national dish is ackee and saltfish, Barbadians enjoy steamed flying fish and cou-cou, pepperpot soup is another tasty dish. The Leeward Islands have a favourite rabbit and groundnut stew. The national dish of Dominica is frogs legs, known as 'mountain chicken'. Trinidadians enjoy Indian-style dishes like roti and Chinese food is also popular.

Products for export

Look out for these products when you are out shopping:

Tia Maria (liqueur)	Barbados rum
Curacao (liqueur)	Muscavado sugar
Dunns River Produce	Demerara sugar
Creamed coconut	All-spice/Pimento
Havana cigars	Angostura Bitters
Geest bananas	Grace ackee

Fruit and vegetables

This is a list of fruit and vegetables grown in the Caribbean. Look in your local supermarket or green-grocers to see if any of them are on sale. Some products may be found in tins.

cullaloo	a green, spinach-like vegetable
sweet potato	pink-skinned vegetable
yam	brown, rough-skinned vegetable
breadfruit	large, round, green-skinned vegetable
guava	pale yellow-skinned fruit with pink or white flesh
ugli	yellow, coarse-skinned fruit slightly larger than an orange
plantain	large, banana-like vegetable, green or yellow with black shading
pigeon peas (gungo peas)	small purple-grey dried peas
mango	smooth-skinned yellow/red fruit
papaya (paw paw)	yellow or green pear-shaped fruit

Religion

Religion plays a very important part in Caribbean life. People in the Caribbean are lucky because in nearly all the islands religions of all kinds are tolerated and people can worship in any way they choose. Some islands have one main religion while others have many different types. People of different religious beliefs celebrate births and marriages in their own way and have different ceremonies.

Variety of beliefs

Many Caribbean people are Christians. They worship as Roman Catholics, Anglicans, Methodists and Baptists. Hindu children often have a shrine at home, while many Christian children go to Sunday School.

Some young Caribbean Christians belong to the Pentecostal movement. Gospel music plays an important part in their worship. Judaism and Buddhism are also found in the Caribbean.

Old and new faiths

Slaves brought with them their traditional beliefs. Drums and dance were important to African beliefs. Slaves were forbidden to use

The Church of St Thomas the Apostle, Kingston Parish Church, Jamaica.

Pupils from Westwood High School, Jamaica, going to church on Sunday morning. The school operates a rotation system, which means the pupils go to a different church each week of the month. One week they go to the Baptist Church (shown here), the next to the Methodist Church, the next to the Anglican Church and on the fourth Sunday they have a service at school.

A river baptism service of a Pentecostal Church in Jamaica.

A Rastafarian from Jamaica. Rastafarians do not comb or cut their hair. It is washed and styled into 'locks'.

drums because their masters were afraid they would be used to send secret messages. Traditional African worship from the Yoruba religion from West Africa still survives in Haiti, Jamaica, Cuba and Trinidad.

The Rastafarian faith developed in Jamaica in the 1930s. It grew from the writings and speeches of black thinkers and leaders. The most important of whom were Emperor Haile Selassie of Ethiopia and Marcus Garvey (see page 31). The faith has spread to other islands and overseas to the USA and Europe. Most Rastafarians have a strong belief in the Bible. They are usually vegetarians and have rules about how their food is prepared.

There are different groups of Rastafarians.

Some groups see Africa as their spiritual homeland. Rastafarians have developed their own special language and often wear the colours red, gold, green and black as a sign of their links with Africa (see below).

Rastafarian colours and their meaning

RED	for the blood and suffering of the African people.
GOLD	for the wealth of Africa and her sunshine.
GREEN	for the promise of the good life from the land.
BLACK	for pride in the colour of their skin.

Caribbean culture

The different people who have come to live in the Caribbean have all contributed to its rich artistic life and the area is particularly famous for its music. Reggae, calypso, and the steel band all come from the Caribbean.

Making music

People in the Caribbean have always made their own music. Arawak people made drums from hollow logs and whistles out of reeds. Carib people made flutes out of bones and shakers out of dried shells of gourds (large round vegetables). The Africans brought the art of drumming from Ghana. The slaves made musical instruments out of what they could find and people still make their own instruments today. Bamboo flutes are popular as well as whistles, tin cans, gourds and seed pods which are all used as percussion.

In Jamaica and Haiti music has a very heavy African style. On other islands it has a more Spanish flavour. Many European rock musicians use Caribbean recording studios and often copy the local music trying to capture its special sounds. Music is very closely linked to dancing and the Caribbean is famous for the meringue, rumba and cha-cha.

Folk stories

The Caribbean is rich in stories, folk tales and legends. Some are about ghosts and evil spirits and some of the most famous are about

Carnival time in Dominica when music and dancing take place on the streets.

small animals, such as the spider 'Anansi'. He has human characteristics and often gets into trouble. On some islands these are called 'crick crack' stories. Riddles and proverbs are also important in Caribbean folk culture.

28

Haitian paintings for sale. Many show details of Haitian life and history.

Painters

The painters of the Caribbean islands use bright, striking colours to paint people as well as birds, flowers and the seashore. Many artists paint religious stories with African characters. Painters from Haiti are famous around the world and examples of their work can be seen in galleries in Paris and New York.

Writers

Many islands have produced all kinds of writers. There are story writers, historians and biographers. Authors have written in Creole or Patois as well as in English and French. C.L.R. James was born in Trinidad, he has written stories as well as historical works, including a play about Toussaint L'Ouverture. Andrew Salkey's *Hurricane* and Michael Anthony's *Green Days by the River* are both stories about young people growing up in the Caribbean. One other famous writer born in the Caribbean is V.S. Naipaul, an Asian novelist from Trinidad.

A test match between the West Indies and England at Sabina Park, Jamaica.

A statue of a Jamaican athlete outside the National Stadium in Kingston.

Sport

The islands have hosted the Commonwealth Games, and a number of outstanding Caribbean athletes have broken world records in both track and field events. Cricket is the most popular sport in the Caribbean. The West Indies cricket team is ranked amongst the best in the world and has players from many islands and Guyana. Young boys in the Caribbean usually learn to play cricket at school and girls play netball and hockey. Both girls and boys play volley-ball and rounders.

Fishing is also an important sport. Visitors can go deep-sea fishing for sharks, barracuda and marlin. The Cayman Islands (to the north-west of Jamaica) provide good seas in which to catch yellow fin, Bonito and barracuda. Snorkling and scuba diving are very popular ways of exploring the rich Caribbean seas. Other sea sports include windsurfing, waterskiing and sailing.

29

The Caribbean and the world

For many years people from the Caribbean have played an active part in world affairs. During the two World Wars many men from the Caribbean islands came to Europe to fight for Britain.

Most of the Caribbean islands are part of the Commonwealth. This has meant that they have had a special political relationship with Britain and other countries which were British colonies.

Famous people

The Caribbean has produced outstanding people in all walks of life. Many Caribbean nurses still honour the work of Mary Seacole, a Jamaican nurse who lived in the 19th century. She nursed people in the Caribbean

Eugenia Charles, a politician from Dominica.

Mary Seacole (1805-1881).

and Central America and sent to nurse British soldiers during the Crimean War. Marcus Garvey is an important figure in the history of the Caribbean. He said that black people should be proud of their colour and culture. He tried to organise a worldwide movement to improve the status of black people in America and the Caribbean. Hilda Gibbs-Bynoe qualified as a doctor in London in 1951. She went to Trinidad to work in local hospitals and in 1968 she returned to Grenada where she was born, to become the first locally born governor. She was given the honour of Dame of the British Empire by the Queen. Eugenia Charles of Dominica was also honoured by the Queen.

Marcus Garvey (1887-1940)

Europe and America

Since the Second World War many Caribbean people have travelled to Britain to work. They were invited in the 1950s to help ease a labour shortage. They worked in factories, on the transport systems and in hospitals and helped to build the economy. Caribbean people also came to Britain to study. There are many children in Britain today whose parents or grandparents were born in the Caribbean. People of Caribbean descent are playing an increasingly important role in all walks of British life.

The Caribbean also has close links with North and Central America. Men from the islands helped to build the Panama Canal and many worked on farms in the USA in the 1930s and 40s. Many Caribbean people have relatives in the USA, Canada and Britain.

Federation and beyond

On the whole the Caribbean islands, especially the English speaking islands, have quite a lot in common. Jamaica, Trinidad and Tobago, Barbados and others are now independent countries with their own elected governments. In 1958 their governments tried to join together and become a Federation of the West Indies. They thought that they could be more powerful as a Caribbean nation. But the federation did not work and when Jamaica dropped out others followed. The federation was finally dissolved in 1962. Caricom is now the main link between the thirteen English-speaking islands. This organisation was founded in 1973 and one of its aims is to encourage and develop trade between Caribbean countries, including Guyana and Belize. It also encourages co-operation in health and education, and aims to bring about economic unity. The islands are trying to work together to develop themselves as a strong political force.

The Jamaican Conference Centre is used for Caricom meetings. It was opened in 1983 by Queen Elizabeth II.

Index and summary

Population:	33 million (approx)
Main cities:	Havana, Kingston, Santo Domingo, San Juan, Port-au-Prince
Main exports:	Oil, bauxite, bananas, sugar, cocoa, rum, cigars, coffee, citrus fruit, juices, gypsum, petroleum products, vegetables, spices, timber
Main imports:	China, electrical goods, machinery
Currencies:	Various island dollars, US dollar, French franc
Main airlines:	Air Jamaica, BWIA, Caribbean Airways, Cubana, Cayman Airways
Highest point:	Mr Roraima, Guyana
Longest river:	River Essequibo, Guyana
Religion:	Christian, Muslim, Hindu, Jewish, African religions